EXPERIENCING
ISRAEL

TONY EVANS

HARVEST HOUSE PUBLISHERS
EUGENE, OREGON

Photos courtesy of Right Now Media, Pharris Photography, and WikiCommons. Used by permission. Photos courtesy of Getty Images on pgs. 22-23, 26-27 (Jack Sopotnicki); 33 (earthmandala); 34-35 (Zvonimir Atleti); 41 (taln); 63 (trabantos); 82 (rparys); 87 (Robert Huetink); and 88 (Mario Eduardo). Used by permission.
Cover design by Bryce Williamson
Interior design by Dugan Design Group
Cover Photo © Jacek_Sopotnicki, compuinfoto, vvvita, John Theodor, salajean / gettyimages ; Nancy Anderson / Alamy

Experiencing Israel

Copyright © 2020 by Tony Evans
Published by Harvest House Publishers
Eugene, Oregon 97408
www.harvesthousepublishers.com

ISBN 978-0-7369-7566-7 (hardcover)

Library of Congress Cataloging-in-Publication Data

Names: Evans, Tony, author.
Title: Experiencing Israel : walking with Jesus in the Holy Land / Tony Evans.
Description: Eugene, Oregon : Harvest House Publishers, 2020.
Identifiers: LCCN 2019027327 | ISBN 9780736975667 (hardcover)
Subjects: LCSH: Jesus Christ--Travel. | Bible. New Testament--Geography. |
  Israel--Description and travel. | Palestine--Description and travel.
Classification: LCC DS107.5 .E83 2020 | DDC 232.9/01--dc23
LC record available at https://lccn.loc.gov/2019027327

Printed in Korea

20 21 22 23 24 25 26 27 / FCSK / 10 9 8 7 6 5 4 3 2

CONTENTS

WELCOME

Welcome to *Experiencing Israel!*
It is my hope that as you join me
on this virtual visit to the Holy Land, you
will feel as if you have stepped
into the very pages of Scripture.

*One of the ways
we get to know
Jesus better is
by getting to know
the land and culture
in which He lived
and ministered as the
incarnate God.*

As you spend time with these beautiful photos and read the accompanying text, I want you to picture yourself walking in the very places where the stories of the Bible unfolded. Traveling to Israel, even if only through this book, will take you home—to the place where your faith began.

As you turn each page, take a moment to gaze upon the same landscape the disciples saw. Pause to worship God as you look at the places where Jesus and His followers also worshiped or prayed. Listen for the echoes still reverberating down through history. Imagine you are there. Can you hear Him?

I understand that God's voice can grow faint. There's something about our busy days, schedules, and the demands of life that can make the stories of the Bible seem distant, no more than ink on paper. This isn't a confession I am proud to share, but I share it in hopes of encouraging you. I spent more than 12 years in formal biblical training. First, I did my undergraduate studies. Then I got a four-year master's degree from seminary. And finally, I earned a doctorate. But in that time, my enthusiasm for spiritual intimacy waned.

I can look back and remember the passion and hunger with which I began. It consumed me. Yet, despite the depth of my desire, an interesting thing happened over the course of those 12 years. As I studied God's Word more and more, it seemed that my hunger for personal intimacy with God diminished instead of grew. I had replaced relationship with a goal: a degree.

I've talked with others who had the same experience during their seminary training. We spent so much time exploring the details of God's Word that we grew distant from God and how His Word applies to life.

Reading and studying God's Word can become more about information than illumination.

Unfortunately, that doesn't only happen to seminary students. I'm afraid it happens to many of us. We fall into the routine of relegating Bible engagement to something that needs to be checked off a list so we can start the many activities of the day.

But let me ask you a quick question: Think about one of your most meaningful relationships—whether with a friend, spouse, or child. Now, if you were to check in with that person for a prescribed—and probably short—amount of time once or twice a day, and there was no other interaction, would that negatively impact your relationship? Probably so. This is because relationships are built on engagement, shared experiences, emotional bonds, and even just time spent together saying nothing at all.

While we all know this to be true, few of us recognize that this is how we are to approach God's Word. But after all, His Word is alive. We read in the book of John:

> In the beginning was the Word, and the Word was with God, and the Word was God. He was in the beginning with God… And the Word became flesh, and dwelt among us, and we saw His glory, glory as of the only begotten from the Father, full of grace and truth… No one has seen God at any time; the only begotten God who is in the bosom of the Father, He has explained Him (1:1-2,14,18).

Jesus *is* the living Word of God. So where He walked on this earth ought to matter to us. What He saw ought to intrigue us. One of the ways we get to know Jesus better is by getting to know the land and culture in which He lived and ministered as the incarnate God. The closer we get to Jesus relationally, the more vibrant His teachings

I hope you will come to know Jesus more personally and this book will motivate you to spend a greater amount of time with Him.

and the Scriptures will become to us. As we grow in our relationship with Him and abide with Him, the more power, insight, and understanding we gain (John 15:4-9). As Paul wrote,

> You therefore, my son, be strong in the grace that is in Christ Jesus… Consider what I say, for the Lord will give you understanding in everything (2 Timothy 2:1,7).

Thus, my hope for you as we embark on this journey of tracing the pathway of our Savior throughout the land of Israel is that the photos and writing will draw you closer to Him. I hope you will come to know Jesus more personally and this book will motivate you to spend a greater amount of time with Him. Whether that involves meditating on a specific verse during the day, honoring Him with the attention of your heart, praying continually, writing in a journal, or reading Scripture, the *form* is not as important as the *focus*.

Whether you have always wanted to visit the land of Israel but haven't had the opportunity, or you have traveled there before and want to relive the experience through these words and pictures, my prayer is that this book will inspire you afresh on your walk with our Lord. Recently, traveling with a group of around 700 guests on a trip to Israel proved life-transforming for so many of us. Visiting Bethlehem, Capernaum, the Sea of Galilee, Beit She'an, the Mount of Olives, the Southern Steps, and many more places I usually only get to read about invigorated my soul. It infused my spirit with an abundance of peace and delight. I hope that as you move slowly through this book, taking time to really look at each photo and imagine yourself there—as well as ponder my thoughts about each location—you will also experience deeper insights into the Savior and delight in His love for you.

When you set this book down once finished, I pray you will have been inspired, encouraged, refreshed, and empowered to know Jesus more deeply and personally (Philippians 3:7-10). This is God's desire for us (Jeremiah 9:23-24). May it be our aim.

Come walk with me in the land where Jesus walked.

Tony Evans

BETHLEHEM

Church of the Nativity

The entrance into the Church of the Nativity requires each person to stoop, as it is less than five feet tall.

We begin our tour through the sacred sites of Israel at the place where Jesus was born. The Church of the Nativity is built over the grotto where it is believed that the birth of Jesus took place. Getting to this sacred location requires a trip into the Palestinian town of Bethlehem, just south of Jerusalem in the territory known as the West Bank. The town itself towers high with numerous buildings and shops. The streets teem with people. The image you may have in your mind from songs such as "O Little Town of Bethlehem" might have held true in the time of Christ, but today it no longer applies. Close to 30,000 people crowd into the roughly 12-square-mile town.

Once you arrive at the location of Christ's birth, you discover that a large complex of churches has been built over this beloved area. The site is currently home to the Greek Orthodox, Catholic, and Armenian Orthodox churches due to the Treaty of Berlin (1878). All three surround the spot of the Nativity with their own places of worship.

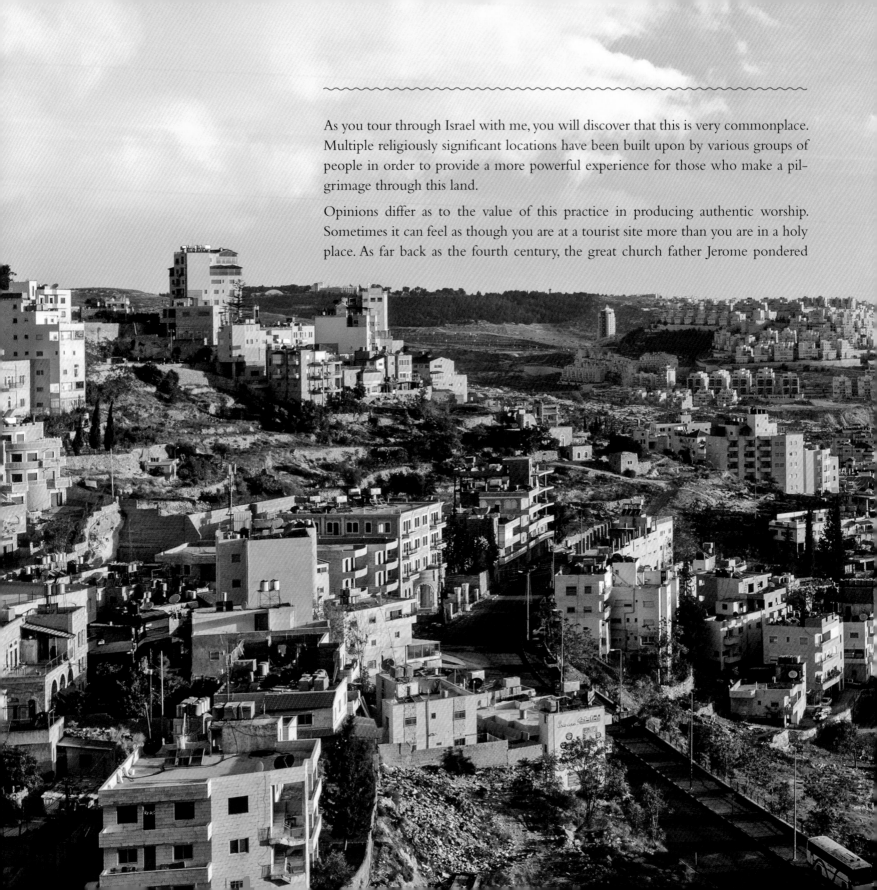

As you tour through Israel with me, you will discover that this is very commonplace. Multiple religiously significant locations have been built upon by various groups of people in order to provide a more powerful experience for those who make a pilgrimage through this land.

Opinions differ as to the value of this practice in producing authentic worship. Sometimes it can feel as though you are at a tourist site more than you are in a holy place. As far back as the fourth century, the great church father Jerome pondered

this very question: "If only I were permitted to look upon that manger in which the Lord lay! Now, as an honor to Christ, we have taken away the manger of clay and have replaced it with crib of silver, but more precious to me is the one that has been removed." Whatever your feelings about the construction of the new settings for the holy sites, true worship can always occur when we align our hearts under God's overarching love. True worship can take place in any place as we set our minds on the truth of God's Word and invite His presence into our moments in time.

One of today's structures forming the Church of the Nativity was erected by Emperor Justinian in the sixth century and stands as the oldest church in Christian history that's still in use. The emperor had replaced the church built by Constantine the Great and dedicated in AD 339.

The entrance into the Church of the Nativity requires each person to stoop, as it is less than five feet tall. Around AD 1500, this entrance was lowered from its original height in order to prevent looters from coming in with their carts. Regardless of the reason behind it, is it not entirely appropriate to bow upon entering the site where Christ humbled Himself to become a man?[1] Paul described this humbling process in Philippians 2:6-7, writing about Jesus: "who, although He existed in the form of God, did not regard equality with God a thing to be grasped, but emptied Himself, taking the form of a bond-servant, and being made in the likeness of men."

Two of the Gospels give us the narrative of Jesus' birth. Luke 2:7 reminds us that He was born in a manger. Many believe it could have been located in a cave. While the Gospels do not specifically reference a cave, many of the written historical accounts dating as far back as AD 160 do mention a "Nativity cave." The Gospels may have omitted this detail since it was so commonplace. And while we may not have the capacity in today's age to determine the accuracy of the statements concerning a cave as Jesus' birthplace, the likelihood of it being true is high. In fact, up through our current time, families who live in the Judean hills might make their homes in primitive dwellings formed in front of natural caves. The caves themselves are then used for storage or to house animals.[2]

Jesus, a unique part of the Godhead, emptied Himself for us when He was made in the likeness of man. Theologians call this the *kenosis*, when deity emptied into humanity. What we had on that first Christmas morning was a baby in a manger who had created His own mother. What we had was a baby in a stable who had created His own stepfather, as well as the donkeys, sheep, and shepherds who surrounded Him. He made the hay on which He slept. He formed the very ground on which His bed was laid (John 1:3; Colossians 1:16-17).

It is one of the most beautiful of all mysteries: On the day Jesus entered our world as a baby, God covered the light of His own existence with the shroud of skin. Jesus became the most unique human being ever to exist.

A new birth in a royal family usually comes with great pomp and fanfare. There is massive media saturation and a lot of celebration. But not in the case of Jesus. He

Her child
was flesh, bones,
sinew, and blood.
Yet He was
also the perfection
of deity.

came as a king, and He could have been born in a castle. Yet the babe was born in a barn to parents who were both unknown and poor, and He arrived with little worldly notice. Nobody sent flowers. No nursemaid helped with His diapers. The few gifts He received would come much later.

Heaven's own heart had beat in the womb of a young woman for the previous nine months. Out of her body came God's omnipotence covered in humanity's limitations.

Her child was flesh, bones, sinew, and blood. Yet He was also the perfection of deity. He felt hunger because He was fully human, yet He would later feed 5,000 because He was fully God (Luke 9:10-17). He grew thirsty because He was fully human, yet He would one day walk on water because He was fully God (John 6:16-21). Raised by a peasant girl and a carpenter, He grew in knowledge (Luke 2:52), yet He also knew what others thought (Matthew 9:3-4). His mother was a virgin named Mary. In Bethlehem, deity wore a diaper when God took on human flesh.

Through His birth and incarnation, Jesus made it possible for us to get to know Him and learn from Him. He made Himself accessible to us. He was Immanuel, "God with us" (Matthew 1:23). To have God with us means that He is available to every man and woman who comes to Christ. To come to Christ is to have the incarnation operating inside of you, your world, and your circumstances. In the incarnation of Jesus Christ, the supernatural took its place with the natural, making the natural a way to tap into the supernatural. Through Jesus, heaven with all its glory, power, and authority was made manifest on earth. ✡

CAPERNAUM

Ministry and Miracles

Many were brought here from far and wide to meet Jesus, be healed, and receive the comfort they so desperately sought.

Not much has been preserved for us regarding Jesus' childhood or young-adult life. There are only a few stories which give us a glimpse into His growth and development. Luke 2:52 summarizes it this way: "Jesus kept increasing in wisdom and stature, and in favor with God and men." As Jesus grew, His ministry came into being.

The next stop on our tour through Israel takes us to one of the primary locations for Jesus' ministry, as well as the location where He performed many of His miracles. Welcome to Capernaum, a town which uniquely illustrates both the power and love of our Lord.

Capernaum derives its name from a combination of two Hebrew words. The first word is *kaphar*, which means "village." The other word is *Nachuwm*, which honors the prophet Nahum, who began his ministry during the most vile and idolatrous period in the history of Judah, which was ruled by King Manasseh at that time. The situation later improved when King Josiah took the throne. God sent Nahum to condemn Judah's enemy Assyria and its capital city of Nineveh. The fact that God would send a prophet in order to condemn the enemy of a nation whose heart had drifted far away from Him exemplifies the wonder of His grace and love. In fact, Nahum's name literally means "comfort."

Thus, the joining of these two words into *Capernaum* produces a name which symbolically means "the village of comfort." And what a village of comfort it turned out to be. For a period of just under two years, Capernaum became the center of Jesus' early ministry after He was rejected in His hometown of Nazareth. He spent a lot of time here. It was in Capernaum that His public ministry gained momentum. Here, Jesus performed many miracles, including the healing of the centurion's servant (Matthew 8:5-13; Luke 7:1-10); the raising of Jairus' daughter from the dead, along with the healing of the woman with a hemorrhage (Matthew 9:18-26; Mark 5:21-43; Luke 8:40-56); and the healing of the nobleman's son (John 4:46-54).

PIAE · MEMORIAE
R · P · GAVDENTII · ORFALI · O ·
CVIVS · DEVOTA · OPERA
ANTIQVAE · SYNAGOGAE
LAPIDES · SEPTEMTRIONALES
ET · QVATTVOR · COLVMNAE
SVIS · RESTITVTAE · SVNT · SEDIC
OBIIT · DIEBVS · AB · OPERE · SVO · DVG
XII · KAL · MAIAS · A · D · MCMXXI
CONGRESSV · ARCHEOL · INTERNAT · PLAVDENTE
MAGISTRATVS · ANTIQVITATIBVS · CVRANDOS
P

ΗΡΩΔΗCΜΟ
ΜΟΥΚΑΝΟΝ
ΥΙΟCΑΜΑΤΟ
ΤΕΚΝΟΙCΕ
ΓΑΝ
ΤΟΝΚΙΟΝΑ

More miracles were performed here than in any other city. Many were brought here from far and wide to meet Jesus, be healed (Matthew 8:16-17), and receive the comfort they so desperately sought. Yet this comfort didn't always come in a manner they expected. The story captured for us in Mark 2:1-12 provides an example. In this passage we read about the time when a paralyzed man was brought by some of his friends so that Jesus could heal him. But Jesus didn't start out by healing the man's physical issues. Rather, He began by telling the man that his sins were forgiven (verse 5).

While the man and his friends sought a physical cure, Jesus knew a spiritual cure was of greater importance. That's what Jesus addressed first. He wanted to get the man back in spiritual alignment with God before He addressed the physical.

It's like when a child falls off a bike and skins their knee. The parent doesn't automatically apply medication to the open wound in order to promote healing. No, first they have to wash the dirt off the wound and possibly even pick out gravel. Any amount of dirt or gravel, no matter how tiny it is, will only give rise to even larger physical issues down the road. A cleansing must occur before the salve can fully work to produce healing.

Jesus is God's representative to deal with the mire and muck of our sin. It is through the cleansing power of His blood that we discover the cure to anything and everything that seeks to tear us down. See, the devil has a goal. Sin is not some arbitrary, floating mass of germs just waiting for a host. No, Satan tempts us to sin, and he has a distinct goal: death (John 10:10). Satan has come to steal and kill, and he knows that the cost of sin is death (Romans 6:23)—whether it's physical death, relational separation, or emotional death, it doesn't matter to him. But "thanks be to God," for we have overcome the power of death through His Son, Jesus Christ (1 Corinthians 15:57).

Even today when you visit this site, you may become quickly wowed by the modern architecture or the ancient towering columns of religious buildings, and in so doing, miss Jesus altogether.

It was also in Capernaum that Jesus healed the Roman officer's slave from a distance, without even seeing or touching him. Jesus was ministering in Capernaum when the Roman officer sent some Jewish elders and friends to ask Jesus to heal his slave, who was near death. Jesus spoke the healing from where He was, and the slave was immediately restored by the power of His word (Luke 7:1-10). It is this Roman officer to whom tradition attributes the building of the synagogue in Capernaum (verses 4-5).

If you look closely when you visit Capernaum today, you can see the western wall of this first-century synagogue. Underneath the towering white-stone synagogue that was likely built in the fourth century are remnants of the early Roman synagogue made of blackened basalt. If you listen closely, you can hear these remains echoing the history created within them. As we read in Mark 1:21, "They went into Capernaum; and immediately on the Sabbath He entered the synagogue and began to teach."

This small fishing town was once comprised of roughly 1,500 people. Located directly on the banks of the Sea of Galilee, Capernaum was home to many fishermen such as Peter, James, Andrew, and John. In addition, it was a place for trading and commerce as well as a place where a detachment of Roman troops was stationed. Because of this robust trade, tax collectors lived here. One of the tax collectors who made this town his home was Matthew.

Archaeologists have not located Matthew's home, but most believe they have uncovered Peter's actual home, due to writings on the surviving walls. In the fifth century, a church was constructed on top of this site. Centuries later, two-thirds of the entire archaeological area of Capernaum was bought by Franciscans in 1894. The other

third was bought by the Greek Orthodox church. In 1990 a contemporary building was erected over the remains of the fifth-century church, which stood above Peter's home. The main floor of the new building has a glass bottom through which you can view the excavations of Peter's home, the historic location where his mother-in-law was healed (Matthew 8:14-15). This is also presumably a site which became the meeting place for an early Christian house church.

Yet despite this being a place where Jesus' supernatural power and comfort were not only demonstrated but also freely given, many in Capernaum still refused to believe (Matthew 11:23-24). Perhaps they were distracted by the duties or delights of the day. Even today when you visit this site, you may become quickly wowed by the modern architecture or the ancient towering columns of religious buildings, and in so doing, miss Jesus altogether. The ruins from His time on earth must be sought out underneath it all. You have to look for the places where Jesus walked, healed, taught, laughed, and loved. And when you do, you will see Him. "He who seeks finds" (Matthew 7:8). ✡

You have to look for the places where Jesus walked, healed, taught, laughed, and loved. And when you do, you will see Him.

NAZARETH

Synagogue Church

Jesus taught and spoke in many locations during His ministry on earth. One of these locations was the synagogue in Capernaum, which we just visited. Another was a synagogue in Nazareth, Jesus' hometown. Scripture has preserved two such instances of Jesus' work there as a traveling preacher (Luke 4:14–30; Mark 6:1-6). Both times He left an indelible impact on the audience at hand, and not necessarily in the way we might expect.

When Jesus spoke at the synagogue in Nazareth, as recorded in Luke 4, the Jews became so incensed with His interpretation and personal application of Scripture that they literally sought to chase Him out of town. In Mark 6, we see that the locals who had known Jesus as a young boy refused to give Him the credibility He deserved. They questioned, challenged, and insulted Him. To which Jesus replied, "A prophet

However,

the history within

these walls

fills believers

today with an

undeniable sense

of holiness.

is not without honor except in his hometown and among his own relatives and in his own household" (verse 4).

In the place where that synagogue likely stood is a church. It is comprised of a single hall within which stands a solitary cross. Near the cross rests a picture depicting Jesus teaching in the synagogue. The two ancient pillars which frame the small doorway are undated. Crusaders claimed this location in the twelfth century and erected their own church on top of what they believed to be the actual synagogue remains. Nothing can be seen of the original quaint synagogue that served the religious needs of the few hundred Nazareth citizens who lived there during Jesus' lifetime. However, the history within these walls fills believers today with an undeniable sense of holiness. After all, this is the very location where Jesus proclaimed His call to public ministry. This was the site of the inauguration of our Lord as He spoke the truth regarding who He truly was.

> He came to Nazareth, where He had been brought up; and as was His custom, He entered the synagogue on the Sabbath, and stood up to read. And the book of the prophet Isaiah was handed to Him. And He opened the book and found the place where it was written,
>
>> "The Spirit of the Lord is upon Me,
>> Because He anointed Me to preach the gospel to the poor.
>> He has sent Me to proclaim release to the captives,
>> And recovery of sight to the blind,
>> To set free those who are oppressed,
>> To proclaim the favorable year of the Lord."
>
> And He closed the book, gave it back to the attendant and sat down; and the eyes of all in the synagogue were fixed on Him. And He began to say to them, "Today this Scripture has been fulfilled in your hearing" (Luke 4:16-21).

In everyday language, Jesus said, "I am here, and I am He." How will you respond to His timeless message given in the humble synagogue in Nazareth? ✡

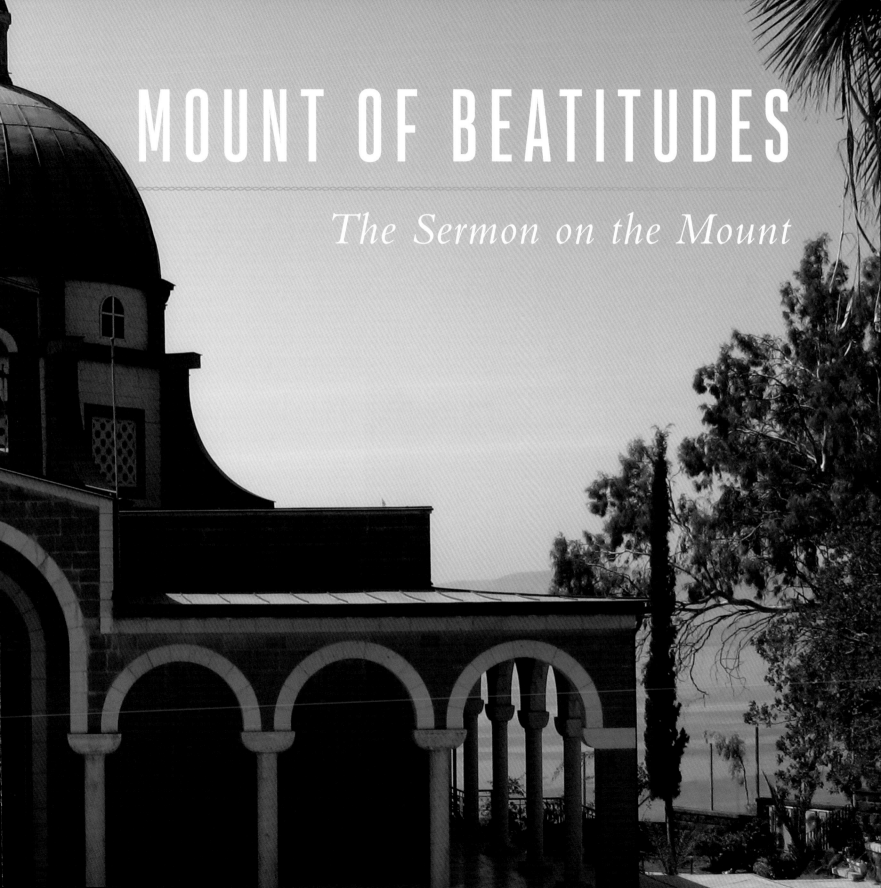

MOUNT OF BEATITUDES

The Sermon on the Mount

*The eight sides
of the octagonal church
symbolize each of the
eight beatitudes Jesus
taught.*

Climbing to the top of the Mount of Beatitudes involves some careful navigating of steep and rugged terrain. But it is worth the effort, as the view from that height will take your breath away. The serenely enchanting Sea of Galilee stretches out before you.

Watching the play of light on the waves caused me to think about the biblical stories that took place on those waters. I couldn't help but feel an overpowering sense of God's presence and peace as I looked on the great body of water upon which Jesus once walked. I couldn't help but feel the strength of His presence when I recalled the time He quieted a violent storm with just His words.

The "mountain" itself is really more of a hillside. Formerly known as Mount Eremos, it lies between Capernaum and Tabgha. When you see the varied terrain that surrounds it, you quickly understand why Matthew spoke of a mountain (5:1) and Luke spoke of more level ground (6:17). One thing that cannot be argued is that there is ample space for a lot of people here. You could easily fit 100,000 individuals in this area without it feeling crowded. Thus, the audience of the Sermon on the Mount could be comfortably seated. And nestled beneath the historic Mount of Beatitudes is the fertile Plain of Gennesaret, where some of Jesus' healings took place.

Not much has been built upon the mountain itself. It has been preserved, to a large degree, as it would have been in Jesus' day. The most significant building, the Church of the Beatitudes, sits near the top and was built for Franciscan Sisters in 1938. The eight sides of the octagonal church symbolize each of the eight beatitudes Jesus taught.

Perhaps on this very spot Jesus offered us the single greatest summation of His teaching on life and love, the Sermon on the Mount. In this lengthy sermon that focused on the centrality and priority of God's kingdom (Matthew 6:33), Jesus spoke of the narrow gate of salvation, the fruit of true followers, the critical importance of obeying God's will, and the need for a sure foundation. He also emphasized that external good works alone do not sanctify a person. God sees the heart and motive. Jesus urged us to remember these right-heart motives when He spoke of the blessings received for embracing the beatitudes, which include living with a poorness of spirit, mourning, being gentle, hungering and thirsting for righteousness, giving mercy, having a pure heart, preserving peace, and accepting persecution on His behalf. These beatitudes illustrate what it looks like to live a life of love for Jesus as expressed in a heart of humility and surrender.

The stillness of this mountain, which you experience when you stand upon it, also serves as a reminder of what Jesus spoke here:

> Beware of practicing your righteousness before men to be noticed by them; otherwise you have no reward with your Father who is in heaven. So when you give to the poor, do not sound a trumpet before you, as the hypocrites do in the synagogues and in the streets, so that they may be honored by men. Truly I say to you, they have their reward in full. But when you give to the poor, do not let your left hand know what your right hand is doing, so that your giving will be in secret; and your Father who sees what is done in secret will reward you. When you pray, you are not to be like the hypocrites; for they love to stand and pray in the synagogues and on the street corners so that they may be seen by men. Truly I say to you, they have their reward in full. But you, when you pray, go into your inner room, close your door and pray to your Father who is in secret, and your Father who sees what is done in secret will reward you (Matthew 6:1-6).

God sees the heart. May this sacred place and the words spoken here always remind us to serve Him with a pure heart, love others unconditionally as He has loved us, and bring Him glory in all we do and say. ✡

SEA OF GALILEE

Calming the Storm

*This remains
a place where many
pilgrims sense
the presence
of Christ.*

Technically, the "Sea" of Galilee is really a freshwater inland lake, about thirteen miles long and seven-and-a-half miles wide at its greatest breadth. Its greatest depth is approximately 155 feet. The hills rise around its perimeter except in the south, where the Jordan River serves as an outlet. In the time of Jesus, the Sea of Galilee (also known as the Lake of Gennesaret) provided a livelihood for fishermen, including many of the original disciples.

This was a place where Jesus demonstrated His power over the natural world by providing miraculous catches of fish (Luke 5:4-11) and calming the stormy sea (Matthew 8:23-27; Mark 4:35-41; Luke 8:22-25). Jesus even walked upon these very waters (Matthew 14:22-33; Mark 6:45-52; John 6:16-21). This remains a place where many pilgrims sense the presence of Christ. It was where the disciples met Him after His resurrection (John 21), and it is where, in our hearts, we might meet Him today.

As you look upon the waters on a calm day, it is hard to imagine the power of the storms that sometimes cause the waves to crash violently. But storms on this sea can arise without much warning. One time when I was out on the Sea of Galilee while on a tour, a storm blew in, and we had to head for shore as quickly as we could.

Life is often like that. Everything may seem peaceful, serene, and safe one moment, and then, in the very next moment, chaos can occur. Our circumstances can change so quickly, causing us to feel as if the waves of worry, doubt, anxiety, and fear are beating at our very souls. In such times, I want to encourage you to remember the normally peaceful state of the Sea of Galilee. For no amount of wind or waves can stand against the power of Jesus' words. When the storms arose in His day, and His disciples were filled with fear, He simply commanded the sea, "Hush, be still," and it was (Mark 4:39). This very day He can command peace into your life if you will call upon Him in your times of need.

Peter is my favorite disciple because he was bold, daring, and confident. But this boldness sometimes got him in trouble. Remember when he asked Jesus if he could also walk on the waves (Matthew 14:28-31)? The request wasn't what did him in. Rather, it was his focus. Once Peter stood on the water and felt the power of the wind's force all around him, he took his eyes off the Lord. As soon as he did, Peter sank. As he sank, he called out, "Lord, save me!" (verse 30).

This is a prayer you can also pray when you feel, like Peter did, that life's storms are too much to bear. You do not need to say an eloquent prayer, just an honest one. And when you do, you can trust that the hand of the Lord will also reach out to lift you up and return you to the safety of His presence and peace, just as He did for Peter. ✡

As you look upon the waters on a calm day, it is hard to imagine the power of the storms...

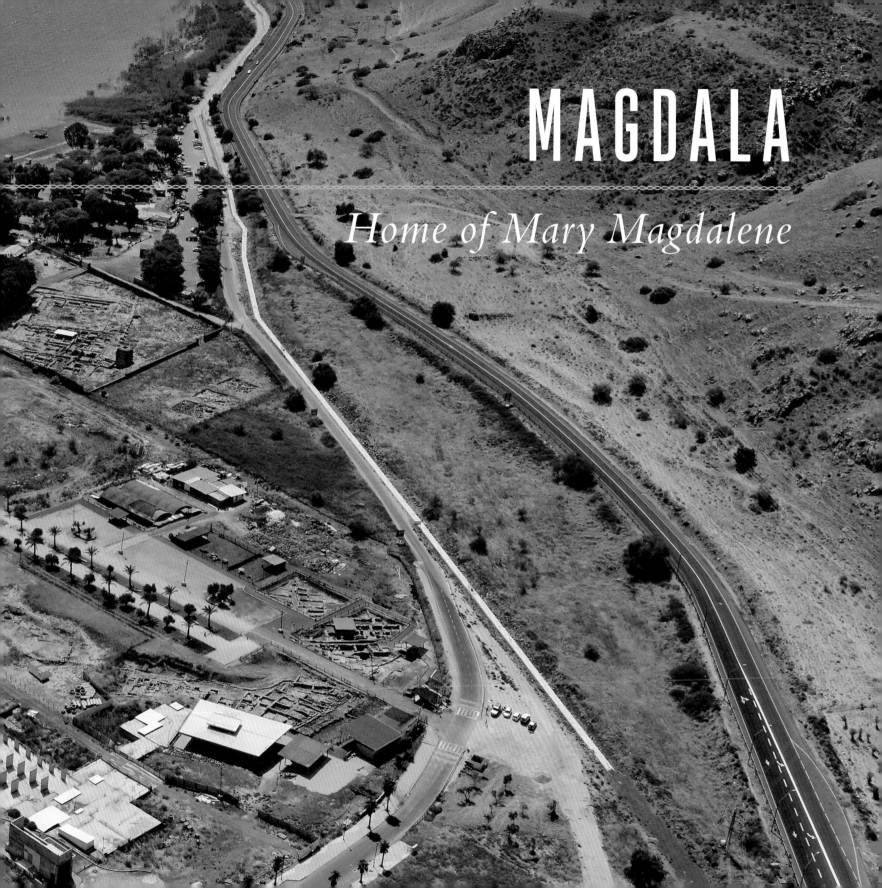

MAGDALA

Home of Mary Magdalene

Walking through the archaeological dig at Magdala gives valuable insight into the culture and lifestyles of a first-century Jewish town.

One of the unsung treasures in Israel, not often among the typical tourist stops, is the synagogue in Magdala. This first-century synagogue is the oldest one discovered in all of Galilee, and it has been dated to the time of Jesus through a coin found inside the remains of its walls that was minted in Tiberias in the year AD 29.

Magdala sits near the present town of Migdal along the western coast of the Sea of Galilee. During the time of Christ, it was a perfect location to catch an enormous supply of fish, for which it was famous. Archaeologists have uncovered the remains of a warehouse placed strategically next to a large stone wharf. Discovering these remains validates the meaning of the town's original name, which was Migdal Nunia (i.e., "fish tower"). At the time, it was the largest city on the west side of the Sea of Galilee.

At some point this town became known as Magdala, which gives the context for how Mary Magdalene came to receive her own name. She was literally known as Mary of Magdala, having been born and raised here.

While Scripture doesn't specifically mention this town, Matthew 4:23 does tell us that Jesus taught in the synagogues throughout the region.

> Jesus was going throughout all Galilee, teaching in their synagogues and proclaiming the gospel of the kingdom, and healing every kind of disease and every kind of sickness among the people.

Thus, Jesus undoubtedly would have taught in this one. In addition, Jesus' tie to Mary Magdalene would have brought Him to this area since it is here that most experts believe He drove out the seven demons that had tormented her (Luke 8:1-3). Although she was clearly an influential and prosperous citizen, she had suffered under demonic oppression. Once Jesus set her free, she committed her life into His service. Due to her connections in this wealthy fishing town, she was able to contribute to the financial needs of Jesus' travels and ministry.

For a woman to receive so much prominence in ministry during biblical days was even more countercultural than it is today.

Many people do not realize the significance of Mary Magdalene in Jesus' life and ministry, but she is mentioned more often in the Gospels than most of the apostles. She was a consistent and important supporter of His ministry needs, as well as a witness to His death and burial (Matthew 27:61; Mark 15:40,47; John 19:25). Not only that, but Mary was also present among the women who first witnessed the empty tomb and received the charge given by the angel to tell others (Matthew 28:1-8; Mark 16:1-8; Luke 24:1-10). She is also singled out in John's Gospel as the first person to see Jesus in His resurrected body, after which she received a personal commission from Jesus to tell the disciples about Him (20:11-18).

For a woman to receive so much prominence in ministry during biblical days was even more countercultural than it is today. Jesus modeled what it looks like to show equality and value to all, in addition to preaching it. In our contemporary culture, we have a ways to go in applying Jesus' validation of both genders for the service of His truth. The scripturally substantiated influential role of Mary Magdalene sheds light on the power of Jesus to stand up against cultural norms. He was a front-runner in tearing down the wall of division between genders, ethnicities, and races. The synagogue at Magdala also serves as a reminder of Jesus' boundless love, His power over spiritual attack, as well as His ability to create transformative life change.

Several mansions have been unearthed in this archaeological dig, revealing Magdala as a hub for wealthy merchants. Three ritual baths were also found, so far dated as the oldest in the country that tap into groundwater. In fact, many of the shops that lined the main paved street were so technologically advanced as to have fresh groundwater piped into them. This plumbing system enabled the sales of fresh fish to expand, making this city a central source of food for neighboring towns.

When you visit Magdala, you can see the only fully uncovered flooring of an actual first-century synagogue in all of Israel. You can also see a replica of what is known as the Magdala Stone, which, on its front and sides, contains possibly the earliest known renditions of the second temple. The back of the stone displays pillars and wheels, as well as an illustration of fire, and likely refers to the Holy of Holies. This beautiful, ornate stone also contains other symbols and a rosette, and archaeologists and theologians are seeking to interpret their meanings. The original stone remains with the Israel Antiquities Authority for its protection until a final location for display is decided.

Walking through the archaeological dig at Magdala gives valuable insight into the culture and lifestyles of a first-century Jewish town. It has been preserved in such a way as to give an authentic glimpse into this time period when Jesus walked on earth. In fact, the synagogue itself is so unspoiled that you can actually see the locations of separate rooms. There is an entrance area, which also could have doubled as a room for study. And there is a chamber where the Torah scrolls would have been kept. Visualizing the activities of the time period as you look upon the synagogue can fill you with reverence for the sanctity of this rare space.

Off to the side of the archaeological dig sits a modern building that you can tour to learn more about the history of the location. It also serves as a place of worship for pilgrims who have made their way here to experience Jesus more fully.[3] ✡

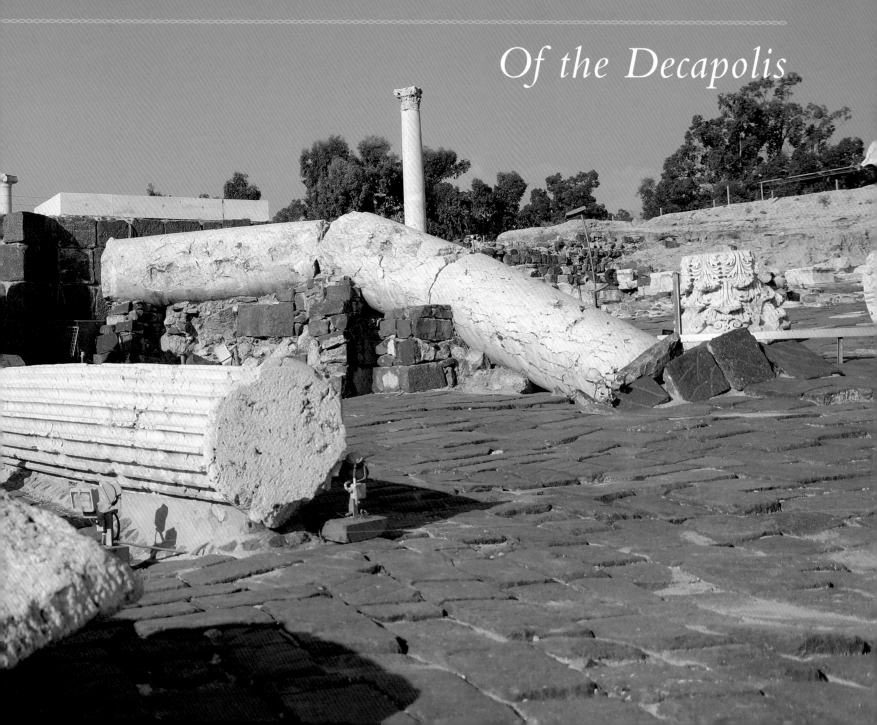

BEIT SHE'AN

Of the Decapolis

A visit to

the ruins here

also gives us

a window into

what a bustling city

looked like in

the time of the

New Testament.

W here now stretches a sprawling national park, there once sat an ancient Roman city. Approximately 20 miles south of the Sea of Galilee, Beit She'an strategically bridges the Harod and Jordan Valleys. Its lush land, fertile soil, and enormous supply of water led the third-century Jewish sage Resh Lakish to say, "If the Garden of Eden is in the land of Israel, then its gate is Beit She'an." The site remains breathtakingly spectacular even to this day. A visit to the ruins here also gives us a window into what a bustling city looked like in the time of the New Testament.

Yet before the Romans conquered this land, it had passed through the hands of many. And after the Romans were forced to let it go, it again passed through the hands of many more. Prior to the Romans, the Canaanites called it home, erecting temples to their gods. At some point, the Egyptians occupied the region. In fact, extensive excavation of one particular ten-acre mound has peeled back the layers of more than 20 ancient civilizations.

In the time of Joshua, the land fell to Manasseh but remained occupied by the Canaanites (Joshua 17:11-12; Judges 1:27). In the time of the kings, Beit She'an was initially controlled by the Philistines and soon became a pivotal historical marker in the process of recapturing the kingdom. When the Philistines found Saul and his three sons among the dead on Mount Gilboa, they used Saul's body as a trophy to display their victory, impaling the former king and his sons on the wall of Beit She'an. Later, the men of Jabesh-gilead retrieved the bodies, burned them, and then buried them in Jabesh (1 Samuel 31:8-13; 1 Chronicles 10:8-12). Yet this momentary Philistine triumph was overturned in David's crowning victory when he was officially declared king.

The city that once stood as a reminder of the Israelites' loss and humiliation returned to Israelite control. King David conquered the city along with Megiddo and Ta'anach. Later, it served as a major administrative center in his son Solomon's kingdom.

Walking through the ruins and reconstructions within this national park instantly whisks you into an era of Roman rule. The nearly 400 acres served as home to the roughly 40,000 citizens who lived here during the time of Roman control. The remnants of public baths appear along the various walkways. Shops for vendors and artisans are outlined in the excavations. A towering colonnade frames the central street,

the columns like vigilant guards on duty. You'll also see the remains of glory dotting the landscape: a gym, paved basalt roads, and exquisite tile. And you can't miss the amazing 7,000-seat theater, which is still in use today, and where I had the privilege of speaking to more than 700 people on our recent tour of Israel.

Being in this region (the Decapolis) where Jesus performed so many great miracles gives us ample reason to worship and to contemplate how His power was manifested while He was on earth (Matthew 4:25; Mark 5:20; 7:31). Knowing that this was the same area where the man delivered by Jesus from the oppression of a "legion" of demons proclaimed what Jesus did for him (Mark 5:5-20) testifies to Jesus' authority over evil spirits and creates a profound sense of comfort and peace. This comfort rests in the assurance of Christ's power over all. Yet it also serves as a powerful motivation to testify to what He has done, and is continuing to do, in our lives today. The conversation and commission preserved for us in Mark 5:18-20 ought to propel us forward to share with others about Jesus' work and power.

> As He was getting into the boat, the man who had been demon-possessed was imploring Him that he might accompany Him. And He did not let him, but He said to him, "Go home to your people and report to them what great things the Lord has done for you, and how He had mercy on you." And he went away and began to proclaim in Decapolis what great things Jesus had done for him; and everyone was amazed.

Jesus desires nothing less from those who follow Him today. Our mission field encompasses the farthest reaches of the world (Acts 1:8), but it also includes where we live, work, and spend our ordinary days. We should testify of His power in our homes, on the job, in our communities, and as we go about our everyday activities. You and I have the same commission given to us as this man who walked the streets of Beit She'an so many years ago, telling of the goodness of Jesus Christ. We are to speak of the great things the Lord has done for us and how He has had mercy on us. When we do this—wherever we are—Jesus will bring glory to Himself through our testimonies of His love and grace.

While Beit She'an may mean "house of rest and tranquility," history tells another story—one of conquests, death, earthquakes, humiliations, destructions, and power struggles. Yet for the believer, the name's meaning rings true. Because, as the demon-possessed man experienced, in this world we may have difficulties, trials, struggles, and trauma—yet Jesus offers both rest and tranquility to any who call on His name (Matthew 11:28). As He has assured us…

> These things I have spoken to you, so that in Me you may have peace. In the world you have tribulation, but take courage; I have overcome the world (John 16:33). ✡

While Beit She'an may mean "house of rest and tranquility," history tells another story…

BETHANY

Tomb of Lazarus

Jesus came that He might give us life, but He also came as the life itself.

While the small town of Bethany sits on the eastern slope of the Mount of Olives, only a few miles away from Jerusalem, it takes a significant amount of time to drive there today. This is due to the "separation wall" which was erected by Israel in the early 2000s. The wall divides the main street of this town, making Bethany a less-visited detour off the beaten track for most tourists and pilgrims. Due to the increased travel distance, as well as the difficulties in crossing the border into the West Bank, you will find this holy place less trafficked when you arrive. As busy as so many of the key sites have become, this is a wonderful treat.

The tomb of Lazarus itself, though, may not be what you imagine from reading John 11:38. It certainly wasn't what I thought it would be when I first visited. The entrance to the tomb starts at street level, and from there you descend a narrow stairwell. Twenty-four uneven steps circle their way into what appears more like a sunken cave than the burial chambers pictured in most Bible illustrations. The entrance to the tomb itself sits as a gaping hole cut directly into the ground, as if waiting to swallow whomever enters. It is accessed by even more steps, which lead you through an even narrower entry into the place where Lazarus' body once rested.

It is believed that Jesus stood at this narrow entrance to the tomb when He called Lazarus to come forth from the grave. Prior to calling him, Jesus revealed an important insight into His identity when He said to Martha that He is "the resurrection and the life" (John 11:25). Jesus spoke these words to His broken friend in the face of her brother's death. Martha had lost all hope and had momentarily forgotten how to

Death is swallowed up in victory.
O death, where is thy sting?
O grave, where is thy victory?

The glory of God shall be seen by those who put
their faith in Jesus in times of greatest distress and
hopelessness. They are certain that He is greater
than any distress, even greater than death itself.

Der Tod ist verschlungen in den Sieg.
Tod, wo ist dein Stachel?
Hölle, wo ist dein Sieg?

Herrlichkeiten Gottes sollen jene schaun,
die in grösster Not und Ausweglosigkeit Jesus
Glauben schenken, gewiss, dass Er immer
grösser ist als jede Not, selbst grösser als der Tod.

believe. Grief can do that to you, can't it? It can cover you with clouds so thick that you no longer recognize where you are. But Jesus comforted Martha in her moment of pain. He reminded her of the ultimate truth, which is that He is the resurrection and the life.

Jesus reminded Martha—and all of us—that when it comes to grief and death, you need more than theology on a shelf. You need *Him*. Just like when you are sick, you don't need a medical book or a medical research website—you need a doctor who can give you medicine. When you are in trouble, you don't need a law book—you need a lawyer. You need the incarnation of the book.

Jesus came that He might give us life, but He also came as the life itself. He is the power of resurrection, and He is life. When you allow life's troubles and trials to drive you to Him, you will come to recognize His power not only to calm you in the midst of chaos, but also to resurrect those things in your life that you thought—beyond a shadow of a doubt—were dead.

This is exactly what Martha did when she allowed the stone to be moved. The removal of the heavy stone opened the doorway to a miracle. The entrance to the tomb had only enough room for one person at a time to enter or exit. Bodies would have been carried into tombs of this nature by one individual holding the front and another holding the feet. But Scripture tells us that Lazarus came out of the tomb in his own strength though still bound by grave clothes (John 11:44). Not only did Jesus raise Lazarus from the dead, but He also gave him the strength he needed to get out of the grave. Seeing the location of this exit from Lazarus' tomb in person only increased the awe and wonder I have for this miraculous event.

Jesus' compassion for Martha and Mary, as well as His desire to honor the Father through signs and wonders, prompted the impossible. The message of this miracle is both simple and profound. Faith must precede sight if we are to experience the supernatural authority of Christ being made visible in our lives. ✡

JERICHO

Rahab, Zaccheus, and Bartimaeus

The story of Joshua and how the walls of Jericho tumbled down is one every child learns in Sunday school, and the account of how God led Joshua to defeat his enemies here is found in Joshua 6. These walls are now gone, but the remnants have been discovered by archaeologists. From the excavations, you can get an idea of what a typical Canaanite city from Old Testament times was like. Jericho was located at a strategic point in the Jordan Valley and thus became an important city.

Rahab hid the Jewish spies in Jericho (Joshua 2), and it was rebuilt in the time of Ahab, one of the worst kings of Israel (1 Kings 16:34). Later, both Elijah and Elisha ministered here (2 Kings 2:4-22). Much later, Herod the Great placed one of his palaces here. Tradition suggests that the temptation of Jesus in the wilderness occurred near Jericho (see the story in Matthew 4:1-11; Mark 1:12-13; Luke 4:1-13), and that this was also where Jesus spotted Zaccheus in a sycamore tree and led him to salvation (Luke 19:1-10). And it was here, on His final trip to Jerusalem, that Jesus healed a man who had been blind (Matthew 20:29-34; Mark 10:46-52; Luke 18:35-43).

Jesus was surrounded by a large crowd on His way out of Jericho when a blind man named Bartimaeus cried out to Him. He was a beggar who depended on others for food and shelter. Thus, when he became aware of Jesus' presence in the vicinity, he persistently called out to Him and begged for something more than food and shelter. He begged for mercy.

It is very likely, since Mark mentions the blind man's family connections in his recording of this incident, that Bartimaeus was from a well-known lineage (10:46). In that day, his social decline from a prominent home to the role of beggar would have made him an outcast. That's why the people tried to silence him. His actions were not seemly. Yet he continued to call out, referring to Jesus as the "Son of David" (verses 47-48). By calling on Him as the Son of David, Bartimaeus let those around him know that he believed Jesus to be the prophesied Messiah who would come and sit on David's throne. Scripture tells us that the people reacted harshly to this man. They didn't merely seek to silence him; rather, they "sternly" attempted to quiet him (verse 48). But as they did, he just cried out even more loudly.

Hearing these cries for mercy, Jesus called for him to come near. Bartimaeus' enthusiasm when called by Christ ought to inspire our own. The Bible records it this way: "Throwing aside his cloak, he jumped up and came to Jesus" (verse 50). This probably brought a smile to our Savior's face. Then, with the tenderness of a loving parent, Jesus healed his eyesight and restored his hope. The man's physical sight now matched his spiritual sight because he was one of the few who truly saw Jesus for who He was.

Just the opposite had engulfed the spiritual leaders of that day as they continued to refuse to believe in Jesus, the Son of David—the promised Messiah. Despite His many signs and wonders which He performed in broad daylight, validating who He was, spiritual blindness plagued most people in that time.

When Bartimaeus was healed, he chose to follow Jesus (Mark 10:52). No doubt this led to a life of service for the one who had made him well. May we also use the life God has given us in order to serve Christ as His followers. And may those of us who have been gifted with spiritual sight (healed from our former blindness and darkness) pray for the salvation of the Jewish people who have yet to embrace the Messiah who loves them so. ✡

Jericho was located at a strategic point in the Jordan Valley and thus became an important city.

JERUSALEM

The City of David

It is no wonder that Jerusalem is considered one of the most sacred places on earth.

Now we come to the great city where the events of Jesus' final days occurred. From a distance you can see the walls surrounding this ancient city, still towering as if seeking to contain the mysteries held within them for ages to come. Jerusalem is considered holy by those of many faiths—including Jews, Christians, and Muslims. It is the central city of the biblical story, and countless important events occurred here. It is "the city which the LORD had chosen…to put His name there" (1 Kings 14:21). David captured Jerusalem, made it his capital, and named it "the city of David" (2 Samuel 5:9). Here David was buried, and the city was expanded and fortified by his son Solomon. It was also here that the first temple was constructed (1 Kings 6–9; 2 Chronicles 3:1).

Jerusalem was restored and rebuilt after the Babylonian captivity (Ezra 1–6; Nehemiah 1–6), and Herod the Great renovated the second temple around 20 BC. By the time of Jesus, Jerusalem had grown. Jesus visited the city regularly, and it was here that He was tried, crucified, and raised from the dead. It is no wonder that Jerusalem is considered one of the most sacred places on earth.

There are so many wonderful sites to explore here that I have decided to walk through a few of the key ones in the following pages.

Southern Steps

The Southern Steps are situated within Jerusalem, but I want to draw special attention to them before we begin our tour through the other highlights of the city. This unique location offers us the only known stones upon which we can be assured that Jesus truly walked. As you stand on the well-worn steps leading up to what used to be the entrance to the second temple, you are literally standing where Jesus stood. Your view may differ a bit from His due to time and cultural changes, but much of the foliage and terrain has remained the same. The land is still similar to what Jesus saw as He stood here so many years ago.

These steps and walls once echoed with the sounds of the Jewish pilgrims as they ascended to the Temple Mount, possibly singing the Psalms of Ascent (Psalms 120–134). My favorite psalm would have reverberated in this very place, as thousands upon thousands of Jewish people in Bible days would have recited it as they made this sacred journey. As I stood there myself, I imagined the power of these words being spoken in unison, drawing down God's divine favor and blessing on individuals, families, Zion, Jerusalem, and all of Israel.

> How blessed is everyone who fears the LORD,
> Who walks in His ways.
> When you shall eat of the fruit of your hands,
> You will be happy and it will be well with you.
> Your wife shall be like a fruitful vine
> Within your house,
> Your children like olive plants
> Around your table.
> Behold, for thus shall the man be blessed
> Who fears the LORD.
>
> The LORD bless you from Zion,
> And may you see the prosperity of Jerusalem all the days of your life.
> Indeed, may you see your children's children.
> Peace be upon Israel! (Psalm 128).

When you hear the line "Israel is the only place on earth where the Bible comes alive,"[4] this particular location loudly affirms that truth. Situated next to the most fought-over piece of land on earth—the former site of the first and second temples and the current site of the Muslim-controlled Temple Mount—the Southern Steps provide the opportunity to literally walk where Jesus walked. We know He ascended and descended these steps on numerous occasions. Luke tells us that Jesus made this walk daily while He was in Jerusalem before His crucifixion and resurrection:

> Now during the day He was teaching in the temple, but at evening He would go out and spend the night on the mount that is called Olivet. And all the people would get up early in the morning to come to Him in the temple to listen to Him (Luke 21:37-38).

One important feature you will notice about the steps as you walk on them is that they are irregular. These intentionally uneven steps forced those who walked on them to pay attention to what they were doing. This helped foster a mind-set of focus and reflection on God, rather than on social engagement or buying and selling in the temple courts. In this way, the ability to "enter His gates with thanksgiving and His courts with praise" (Psalm 100:4) would come more naturally without distractions.

In addition to being a place where Jesus walked, this location serves as the backdrop to many biblical stories. It was likely here, for example, that Peter gave his powerful apostolic message that ushered 3,000 Jewish souls into conversion (Acts 2:38-43). And one of the gates you can see leading up to the temple, known as the Triple Gate, is also likely the "Beautiful Gate" mentioned in Acts 3:1-11, where Peter and John healed a lame man who had been begging. The Triple Gate sits on top of a set of steps, but it was blocked by the Crusaders around AD 1100.

Walking these steps, surrounded by all this rich history, reinvigorated my faith. I had the treasured opportunity to address our tour group during the final night of our visit in the Holy Land as they gathered on the very steps where Jesus once stood. The power of that evening and its impact on my spiritual life remains with me to this day. It is my hope that as you look at the images from this location, you will also gain a sense of the Lord's presence and power in your own life. May this prompt you to pray for others to come to know Jesus as their Lord and Savior too.

Temple Mount

What is now the site of the Islamic Dome of the Rock was originally the location of the Jewish temple. The Dome of the Rock sits on the other side of the wall that is above the Southern Steps. The original temple built by Solomon was destroyed during the invasion of the Babylonians in 586 BC and rebuilt around 515 BC by Jewish exiles who returned to the land. King Herod the Great expanded and enhanced this second temple during his reign (37–4 BC). Tradition also suggests that when Abraham prepared to offer Isaac as a sacrifice (Genesis 22), it was upon this very spot.

In New Testament times, the reconstructed temple was a natural place for people to gather, and it was a place where Jesus, Peter, and John all taught (Matthew 21:14-15,23; 26:55; Acts 2:46-47; 3:11; 4:1-2; 5:20-25). In AD 70, the Romans sacked the temple, reducing it to rubble.

Western Wall

As you wander the narrow streets of Jerusalem after visiting the Southern Steps, you will likely find yourself at what is commonly known as the Western Wall. You may have seen this in photos of Israel or if you have visited the country yourself. It is a very well-recognized location because of the pictorial exposure it has received over the years. This is where the Jewish people come to pray on a regular basis. Of note is the dividing wall that separates the men from the women. Each gender must offer their prayers in their own designated section.

Around the wall, you'll find Jewish people praying and worshiping. Since this wall is the only remaining element of the first-century temple, it is considered the holiest place on earth for observant Jews. They believe that the special presence of God, which could be found in the temple, has never left this spot. Christians often pause at the wall and offer a prayer of their own, possibly even reciting the prayer that Solomon lifted to God at the time of the dedication of the first temple (2 Chronicles 6:13-42). Some, like me, also choose to ponder Hebrews 10:1-18 as they pray, considering how the sacrifice of Jesus contrasts with those offered at the temple.

Pool of Bethesda

The Pool of Bethesda is now part of the compound of Saint Anne's Church, which is one of the most beautiful churches in Jerusalem. It was at one of these pools that Jesus met and healed a man who had been unable to walk for 38 years (John 5:1-15).

Via Dolorosa

The Via Dolorosa, "the way of sorrows," attempts to trace the steps of Jesus during the final hours of His life. Today these winding streets offer shopping options similar to those in Jesus' day. Marketplace vendors sell bread, beans, and other food items. Children walk the Via Dolorosa as they go to school. If you are there early in the morning, a quiet hush rests upon these streets, but it soon turns into a frantic bustle as the shops open and the vendors sell their wares.

For those seeking to trace Jesus' steps, 14 stations have been marked along the way, each one commemorating a key moment from when Jesus walked toward His death. While most of the stations are biblical, a few are part of later traditions. Since the early days of the church, many Christians have found it a life-changing experience to trace these steps and ponder our Lord's great love.

Upper Room

The official name for this location is the Cenacle. It is located on the upper floor of a two-story building just south of the Zion Gate. Situated in Jerusalem's Old City, this popular spot draws many people. Due to political controversies between the Jews and Muslims (both of whom view it as sacred for their own reasons), visiting for any length of time isn't always an easy option. But even a quick peek can remind you that this is a special place.

It should be pointed out, though, that archaeologists are not certain that this is the exact location of Jesus' last supper. Another possible location is in what is now the Syrian Orthodox Church of Saint Mark. Many Christian historians believe the Upper Room was probably located in the home of Mary, the mother of John Mark. Yet whether the Cenacle location is accurate or not, visiting allows you the opportunity to reflect on the power of what took place here.

Many significant things happened in the Upper Room, such as Jesus washing His disciples' feet, as He's talking about abiding and servanthood (John 15), sharing the Passover with them, and offering His high priestly prayer. It was the place where Jesus appeared to the disciples after His resurrection (John 20:19-29). And it is in this same location that Jesus promised His disciples that He would send a Helper, the Holy Spirit, to empower them.

During His last supper with them before His arrest, Jesus said, "It is for your benefit that I go away, because if I don't go away the Counselor will not come to you. If I go, I will send Him to you" (John 16:7 HCSB). This very location also served as the scene of the Holy Spirit's coming, which unfolded into the events surrounding the birth of the church on the day of Pentecost (Acts 1:13; 2:1-4).

It's unlikely that the disciples fully understood what Jesus had meant by that statement in John 16:7, when He told them He would go away. Yet by the time He spoke the words "You will receive power when the Holy Spirit has come on you" (Acts 1:8 HCSB), they were paying attention. They may not have fully understood all it meant, but they were beginning to realize His role as King and Messiah meant something far different from what they previously had thought. They asked about the restoration of God's kingdom (verse 6), but Jesus only responded with the promise that God's Spirit would rest on them and that He would impart to them the power of the kingdom.

Jesus' ascension after His resurrection initiated the age of the Holy Spirit. And while it surely must have broken the disciples' hearts to lose one they loved so dearly, the presence of the Spirit would ultimately be better for them—and for us. "How can this be?" some might ask. It's because when Jesus was here on earth, His actions were limited by His humanity. Neither His deity nor His essence were diminished, yet He could only be in one location at a time. When people needed Jesus, they had to meet Him face-to-face.

Now, since the Holy Spirit lives within each follower of Jesus Christ, He goes with us wherever we go. He is always present in full power within each of us, all at the same time. The Holy Spirit is not subject to the limitations of human flesh to which Jesus voluntarily surrendered.

The Holy Spirit is God, the third member of the Trinity, but He often gets little recognition. Some people wrongly assume He does the least of any member of the Trinity. In many circles, the Holy Spirit is only loosely acknowledged, yet it is He who indwells, transforms, and empowers each believer to live the victorious kingdom life. The Holy Spirit provides power for us to function as we align ourselves under the lordship of Jesus Christ. As I stood in the Upper Room, I was reminded of the gift of the Spirit given to every believer.

Garden of Gethsemane

The Garden of Gethsemane is a very special place. Located on a slope of the Mount of Olives, not too far from the Kidron Valley, sits the garden of our Lord. While most of us attach the events of the evening before His crucifixion to this specific location, Jesus actually went here on many occasions with His disciples (John 18:2). In fact, that is how Judas knew where Jesus would be on the night he betrayed Him.

You can enter the garden through the Church of All Nations and explore the place where Jesus prayed earnestly after the last supper as He prepared Himself for betrayal and arrest (Matthew 26:36-56). The garden itself is lovely and peaceful, filled with gnarled and ancient olive trees. It is a great place to meditate on those final moments when Jesus surrendered Himself to the pain and suffering of the cross, praying, "My Father, if this cannot pass away unless I drink it, Your will be done" (verse 42).

Olive trees have a very long life span. A few of the olive trees in the garden today have been in existence for hundreds of years. Many have been dated to the twelfth century. History has recorded that many of the trees around Jerusalem were cut down by the Romans when they conquered the city in AD 70. But whether or not these trees came after Jesus' time in the garden or were actually there when He prayed, they stand tall today as a reminder and a testament to what took place in this sacred location.

One of the most interesting things about olive trees is that if they are nurtured correctly, they can produce olives for hundreds of years. On our group's visit to the Garden of Gethsemane, I saw these massive trees still producing olives. One reason they are able to do so is because their roots go far. These olive trees serve as a life lesson on the importance of having roots and stability. Only then can you bear the best fruit for the kingdom.

Jesus' own stability was tested in this very garden, but He proved Himself able. Scripture tells us that our Savior agonized so greatly that drops of blood came from Him. Luke 22:44 puts it this way: "Being in agony He was praying very fervently; and His sweat became like drops of blood, falling down upon the ground." Yet despite His own despair, Jesus made it His aim to surrender to the Father's will. He gave His life as a living symbol of what Gethsemane means, which is "oil press." Through His willing surrender on the cross, Jesus allowed Himself to be pressed beyond what anybody could bear, and in emptying Himself, He gave us the pathway to our Father in heaven (Philippians 2:7-8).

Church of the Holy Sepulchre

Two locations in Jerusalem lay claim to being the place where Jesus was buried. We'll visit both during our tour. The first is the Church of the Holy Sepulchre, and most archaeologists place this site outside the city walls during the time of Jesus. The tomb itself has not been found, but similar, authentic first-century tombs do exist here. These burial shafts, known as *kokhim*, reveal to us what a typical tomb looked like when Jesus died.

As with many of the holy sites, this one has changed hands over the centuries. Upon Constantine's conversion in the fourth century, he had the pagan temple that stood near this location destroyed and a church erected in its place. The Persians then destroyed that church in the seventh century. In AD 1009, the Egyptians destroyed what had been rebuilt in its place. Then the Crusaders built again upon this land, and what they erected still stands today.

When you first walk up to the entrance of the enormous building, you will spot a ladder sitting on a ledge in the upper window. Because of the Status Quo of Holy Land Sites set forth in 1757, no one is allowed to remove the ladder without the permission of all six of the involved ecumenical Christian orders agreeing to it. The ladder, therefore, has remained essentially right in that place for several hundred years!

Immediately upon entering the church you will find a large stone slab upon which worshipers often place their hands as they kneel and pray. The stone is significant because it is believed by some to be one on which Jesus would have been laid when they took Him down from the cross. However, this specific stone is actually dated to the nineteenth century.

Not only is Jesus' burial tomb thought to be located at this site, but many believe that the traditional place of the cross was situated here as well. You can see the rocky remains of what many call "Golgotha" on the ground floor, preserved behind glass. As you first enter the church, a stairwell to the right of the door will take you up to a floor that sits level with the top of Golgotha.

The Church of the Holy Sepulchre is a heavily trafficked area every day. I was able to visit it on a couple occasions during our group's recent trip to Israel and had the joy of arriving before sunup to a mostly empty site. As I walked the corridors of this

grand structure, I marveled at the variety of worship spaces and chapels—more than 30 different locations—set up by various faiths and denominations. Some are immense. Others are small. Incense and candles burn throughout. The various languages of worshipers fill the air, intermingling.

The enormousness of the church, along with the abundant varieties of worship, may overwhelm Western visitors at first. It looks nothing like our usual conception of either Golgotha or the tomb of Christ based on what we have been exposed to in historical reimaginings of both places. But if you will pause to reflect upon the magnitude and sacredness of what both events—the crucifixion and resurrection of Jesus—mean to you and to all creation, you may be drawn into the presence of God in such a way as you have never experienced before. In doing so, you can gain insight into the breadth of our Lord's saving love, which reaches out to and embraces all people, no matter their background, who choose to place their faith in Him alone for the forgiveness of their sins.

*If you will pause
to reflect upon the magnitude
and sacredness of what
both events—the crucifixion
and resurrection of Jesus—
mean to you and to all
creation, you may be drawn
into the presence of God in
such a way as you have never
experienced before.*

Garden Tomb

Our final stop in Jerusalem is one that is often the most anticipated by first-time visitors to the Holy Land—as it commemorates the place where Jesus was buried and where He rose again. While most scholars consider the environs of the Church of the Holy Sepulchre to be the more likely place where Jesus' death and resurrection occurred, in recent times the Garden Tomb has become a cherished spot to celebrate these events. Whichever is the authentic location, the Garden Tomb remains a tranquil place to ponder what Jesus did for us and how His resurrection changed everything. This is a special spot—a place for prayer and contemplation and celebration.

Located just outside the Old City walls of Jerusalem, this treasured spot welcomes visitors from around the world to pay homage to our Lord and Savior. Although this particular site was not discovered until the late 1800s, it has become popularized over the years through photos and visitors' accounts. It offers a beautiful, landscaped gathering area for tour groups who want to hold a worship service on the grounds. Our group was able to celebrate our Lord here through communion, singing, and preaching during our recent visit.

Pilgrims can actually enter the tomb itself, which symbolically displays the burial place of our Savior (John 19:41; Matthew 27:57-61; Luke 23:50-55). Reflections on His life, death, and resurrection give rise to life-transforming thoughts of adoration and worship. The well-manicured grounds surrounding the tomb give ample space for lingering in this spot, which serves as a beautiful reminder of Jesus' greatest sacrifice on our behalf and His victory over death. As you stand in the midst of these gorgeous gardens, it is easy to recognize that God loves you so much that He stepped out of heaven in the person of Jesus Christ and took the penalty of death in your place on Calvary. Jesus hung on the cross, not for His own sin, but for yours and mine. Because Jesus Christ is without sin, His death paid the penalty for all of us (2 Corinthians 5:21).

People like to call Jesus a good teacher and a great prophet, but His resurrection places Him in a class all by Himself.

Yet some people still wonder how we know that Jesus' death on the cross really took care of our sin problem. We know because of what happened that Sunday. When Mary Magdalene came to Jesus' tomb that morning, she couldn't find Him. She saw someone and thought it was a gardener. She asked Him where the Lord's body had been taken. When the gardener said her name, Mary gasped in amazement. It was Jesus (see John 20:1-18).

She was the first of many witnesses. In fact, according to 1 Corinthians 15:6, more than 500 people personally saw the risen Christ before He ascended into heaven. If not for the resurrection, our faith would be empty and useless. As the apostle Paul said, if Jesus were not raised, we should be the most pitied people on earth. But the fact is, the Lamb of God *has* been raised (1 Corinthians 15:12-20). Jesus Christ delivered death its deciding blow.

People like to call Jesus a good teacher and a great prophet, but His resurrection places Him in a class all by Himself. He is the risen Lord. And because of that, He is the only one through whom salvation can be granted.

After all, you cannot place living faith in a dead savior.

Paul wrote, "If Christ has not been raised, then our proclamation is without foundation, and so is your faith" (1 Corinthians 15:14 HCSB). Without the resurrection, we would still be dead in our sins.

You may have lived a very good life, but "very good" is not good enough. Think about it like an omelet. If you take three good eggs and mix them with one rotten one to cook an omelet, what do you have? Do the three good eggs make the rotten one taste any better? No, the rotten one taints the other three. So it is with sin. On your best day, you still sin (Romans 3:23). You can go to church continually, sleep at the church, eat in the church, do your work at the church, and die in the church, but that is still not good enough to satisfy a holy God. Only Christ's death *and resurrection* count.

Notice that I emphasized "and resurrection." The death of Jesus is important, but so is His resurrection. Too many people try to lessen its significance.

If the resurrection didn't matter, then the stone would have stayed right where it had been placed. But we see in Matthew 28:2 that the angel of the Lord rolled away the stone. The angel didn't roll it away so Jesus could get out. Jesus had already risen! Locked doors were no longer a barrier for Him (John 20:19), so He certainly didn't need help exiting a grave.

No, the angel of the Lord rolled away the stone to show that the tomb was empty and Jesus is alive. God wanted us to see that evil had lost its victory because Jesus had defeated the grave.

If you come looking for Jesus when you visit the Garden Tomb, you will discover, like all the others who seek Him, that He is not here. Praise God, He is not in the tomb.

Mount of Olives

The last stop on our journey is the Mount of Olives, a two-mile-long ridge that lies just east of the Old City of Jerusalem, as if serving as a gateway to the cherished city. The area gets its name from the olive groves that once covered it.

When you stand on the mountain, you are treated to a majestic view of the city. It is a wonderful place to contemplate the events that took place in and around Jerusalem. This was the place from which Jesus looked out over Jerusalem and wept for the city and His people (Luke 19:41-44). From here, He also pondered its prophetic future (Matthew 24–25; Mark 13), and from here, He ascended into heaven (Acts 1:6-12). Zechariah prophesied of a time when the Messiah will stand upon the Mount of Olives, and the mountain will be split in two (14:3-5).

Yet Jesus' ascension is what I want us to focus on as we come to the end of our journey through the Holy Land. Let us not be like His disciples, who required multiple lessons and much exposure to His teachings before finally letting it all soak in to affect their behavior. After all, before the time of His ascension, the disciples had been with Jesus for three years of solid training. They had seen Him perform miracles. Witnessed Him calm the storms. Heard Him teach. Yet when we look at the disciples' behavior during Jesus' trial and crucifixion, it wouldn't appear they had heard or seen much at all.

They doubted Him. Wandered away from Him. Feared others. And they ran.

Yet after their friend and Savior rose from the dead, everything changed. For 40 days, Jesus spoke to them and gave them a crash course on the kingdom of God (Acts 1:3). I suspect the disciples absorbed more in those 40 days than in their previous three years with Jesus. Suddenly He had their undivided attention.

If your doctor were to lecture you about how to manage an illness you didn't have, you might listen…somewhat. More likely, your eyes would glaze over, and his words

*No one else
has ever ascended
from this earth
the way Jesus did,
and no one is
coming back the
way He is
coming back.*

would fall on deaf ears. Yet if you had been diagnosed with that same illness, you would strive to remember every word. And you would apply those words diligently.

I don't doubt the disciples listened closely as Jesus was about to ascend into heaven. His words at this point became very dear to them. That's how it should be for us too. What Jesus taught His disciples before His ascension mattered to them. The life and words of Jesus had become the passion of their lives, and they should be our passion as well.

Luke records the ascension for us in Acts 1:9-10:

> After He had said these things, He was lifted up while they were looking on, and a cloud received Him out of their sight. And as they were gazing intently into the sky while He was going, behold, two men in white clothing stood beside them.

Notice the verbs Luke uses in this passage to describe Jesus' ascension into heaven.

- *He was lifted up.*
- *A cloud received Him.*
- *He was going.*

In other words, Jesus' ascension was visible and physical. This was neither a mirage nor a figment of their imagination. It was a tangible, visible event. In the same way that Jesus was resurrected bodily, He ascended bodily.

It's important to realize Jesus physically ascended—not just as a spirit—and He will also physically return. As the disciples watched Jesus ascend, two angels told them, "This Jesus, who has been taken from you into heaven, will come in the same way that you have seen Him going into heaven" (Acts 1:11 HCSB).

No one else has ever ascended from this earth the way Jesus did, and no one is coming back the way He is coming back. He is the distinct and unique message of all creation.

A day is coming when we will experience a real transformation. This incredible change will occur when Jesus Christ returns for His followers, and we will be with Him forever. Jesus used the image of a wedding to teach about His return (Matthew

25:1-13). At the return of Christ, His followers will take part in a great marriage feast (Revelation 19:6-10). This wedding imagery is so fitting, for one day Jesus will return for us, His bride. One day the trumpet will sound, announcing that Jesus, our Bridegroom, is on His way. And we can anticipate that moment with delight.

Until then, let us press on in our devotion and service to our Lord Jesus Christ. After all, God "made us alive with the Messiah even though we were dead in trespasses. You are saved by grace!" (Ephesians 2:5 HCSB). ✡

FINAL THOUGHTS

I hope you have enjoyed this whirlwind trip through the Holy Land, walking along with me through words and pictures in the very places where Jesus walked. I sincerely hope, if you have not had the chance already, you can trace these steps for yourself someday, stopping to pray, to praise, and to ponder what Jesus did to secure our salvation. Until then, I hope this virtual tour has served as a reminder of a story that isn't just some ancient legend, but that really happened in a real place at a particular time in history. These events mean as much to you and me today as they did when they first took place.

If the stories of Jesus are a little more concrete for you after reading this book, then I have fulfilled my goal. For the whole point in experiencing Israel is to experience Jesus again in a fresh and powerful way. The one in whose footsteps we walked throughout this journey is the one who walks beside you every day. And that reality changes everything! ✡

ACKNOWLEDGMENTS

I want to thank my friends at Harvest House Publishers for their long-standing partnership in bringing my thoughts, study, and words to print. I particularly want to thank Bob Hawkins for his friendship over the years, as well as his pursuit of excellence in leading his company. I want to publicly thank Terry Glaspey, Betty Fletcher, and Amber Holcomb for their editorial efforts. I also want to thank the photographers, Joshua Pharris, Lyndsey McNally, and the RightNow Media film crew led by producer Phil Warner. In addition, my appreciation goes out to Heather Hair for her writing and research in collaboration on the content of this book.

THE URBAN ALTERNATIVE

The Urban Alternative (TUA) equips, empowers, and unites Christians to impact individuals, families, churches, and communities through a kingdom agenda worldview. In teaching truth, we seek to transform lives.

The core cause of the problems we face in our personal lives, homes, churches, and societies is spiritual; therefore, the only way to address it is spiritually. We've tried a political, social, economic, and even a religious agenda. It's time for a kingdom agenda—the visible manifestation of the comprehensive rule of God over every area of life.

The unifying, central theme of the Bible is the glory of God and the advancement of His kingdom. This is the conjoining thread from Genesis to Revelation—from beginning to end. Without that theme, the Bible might look like disconnected stories that are inspiring but seem to be unrelated in purpose and direction. The Bible exists to share God's movement in history to establish and expand His kingdom, highlighting the connectivity throughout, which is the kingdom. Understanding that increases the relevance of these ancient writings in our day-to-day living because the kingdom is not only then—it is now.

The absence of the kingdom's influence in our own lives and in our families, churches, and communities has led to a catastrophic deterioration in our world.

- People live segmented, compartmentalized lives because they lack God's kingdom worldview.

- Families disintegrate because they exist for their own satisfaction rather than for the kingdom.

- Churches have limited impact because they fail to comprehend that the goal of the church is not to advance the church itself, but the kingdom.

- Communities have nowhere to turn to find real solutions for real people who have real problems, because the church has become divided, ingrown, and powerless to transform the cultural landscape in any relevant way.

The kingdom agenda offers us a way to live with a solid hope by optimizing the solutions of heaven. When God and His rule are not the final and authoritative standard over all, order and hope are lost. But the reverse of that is true as well—as long as we have God, we have hope. If God is still in the picture, and as long as His agenda is still on the table, it's not over.

Even if relationships collapse, God will sustain you. Even if finances dwindle, God will keep you. Even if dreams die, God will revive you. As long as God and His rule guide your life, family, church, and community, there is always hope.

Our world needs the King's agenda. Our churches need the King's agenda. Our families need the King's agenda.

In many major cities, drivers can take a loop to get to the other side of the city without driving straight through downtown. This loop takes them close enough to the city to see its towering buildings and skyline, but not close enough to actually experience it.

This is precisely what our culture has done with God. We have put Him on the "loop" of our personal, family, church, and community lives. He's close enough to be at hand should we need Him in an emergency, but far enough away that He can't be the center of who we are.

Sadly, we often want God on the loop of our lives, but we don't always want the King of the Bible to come downtown into the very heart of our ways. Leaving God on the loop brings about dire consequences, as we have seen in our own lives and with others. But when we make God and His rule the centerpiece of all we think, do, and say, we experience Him in the way He longs for us to.

He wants us to be kingdom people with kingdom minds set on fulfilling His kingdom purposes. He wants us to pray as Jesus did—"Not My will, but Yours be done" (Luke 22:42)—because His is the kingdom, the power, and the glory.

There is only one God, and we are not Him. As King and Creator, God calls the shots. Only when we align ourselves underneath His comprehensive authority will we access His full power and authority in our lives, families, churches, and communities.

As we learn how to govern ourselves under God, we will transform the institutions of family, church, and society according to a biblically based, kingdom worldview. Under Him, we touch heaven and change earth.

To achieve our goal, we use a variety of strategies, approaches, and resources for reaching and equipping as many people as possible.

BROADCAST MEDIA

Millions of individuals experience *The Alternative with Dr. Tony Evans*, a daily broadcast playing on nearly 1,400 radio outlets and in more than 130 countries. The broadcast can also be seen on several television networks, online at TonyEvans.org, and on the free Tony Evans app. More than ten million message downloads occur each year.

LEADERSHIP TRAINING

The *Tony Evans Training Center (TETC)* facilitates educational programming that embodies the ministry philosophy of Dr. Tony Evans as expressed through the kingdom agenda. The training courses focus on leadership development and discipleship in five tracks:

- Bible and theology
- personal growth
- family and relationships
- church health and leadership development
- society and community impact

The TETC program includes courses for both local and online students. Furthermore, TETC programming includes course work for nonstudent attendees. Pastors, Christian leaders, and Christian laity, both local and at a distance, can seek the Kingdom Agenda Certificate for personal, spiritual, and professional development. Some courses qualify for continuing education credits and will transfer for college credit with our partner schools. For more information, visit TonyEvansTraining.org.

Kingdom Agenda Pastors (KAP) provides a viable network for like-minded pastors who embrace the kingdom agenda philosophy. Pastors have the opportunity to go deeper with Dr. Tony Evans as they are given greater biblical knowledge, practical applications, and resources to impact individuals, families, churches, and communities. KAP welcomes senior and associate pastors of all churches. KAP also offers an annual summit, held each year in Dallas, Texas, with intensive seminars, workshops, and resources.

Pastors' Wives Ministry, founded by Dr. Lois Evans, provides counsel, encouragement, and spiritual resources for pastors' wives as they serve with their husbands in ministry. A primary focus of the ministry is the KAP Summit, which offers senior pastors' wives a safe place to reflect, renew, and relax along with training in personal development, spiritual growth, and care for their emotional and physical well-being.

COMMUNITY IMPACT

National Church Adopt-a-School Initiative (NCAASI) prepares churches across the country to impact communities through public schools, effecting positive social change in urban youth and families. Leaders of churches, school districts, faith-based organizations, and other nonprofit organizations are equipped with the knowledge and tools to forge partnerships and build strong social service delivery systems. This training is based on the comprehensive church-based community impact strategy conducted by Oak Cliff Bible Fellowship. It addresses such areas as economic development, education, housing, health revitalization, family renewal, and racial reconciliation. NCAASI assists churches in tailoring the model to meet the specific needs of their communities, while addressing the spiritual and moral frame of reference. Training events are held annually in the Dallas area at Oak Cliff Bible Fellowship.

Athlete's Impact (AI) exists as an outreach both into and through sports. Coaches are sometimes the most influential factor in young people's lives—even more than parents. With the rise of fatherlessness in our culture, more young people are looking to their coaches for guidance, character development, practical needs, and hope. Athletes (professional or amateur) also influence younger athletes and kids. Knowing this, we equip and train coaches and athletes on how to live out and utilize their God-given roles for the benefit of the kingdom. We aim to do this through our iCoach app and other resources, such as *The Playbook: A Life Strategy Guide for Athletes.*

Tony Evans Films ushers in positive life change through compelling short videos and feature-length films. We seek to build kingdom disciples through the power of story. We use a variety of platforms for viewer consumption and have received more than 35 million digital views. We also merge film with relevant Bible study materials to bring people to the saving knowledge of Jesus Christ and to strengthen the body of Christ worldwide. Tony Evans Films released its first feature-length film, *Kingdom Men Rising*, in partnership with LifeWay Films in April 2019, with showings in more than 800 theaters nationwide.

RESOURCE DEVELOPMENT

We foster lifelong learning partnerships with the people we serve by providing a variety of published materials. Dr. Evans has published more than 100 unique titles (booklets, books, and Bible studies) based on more than 40 years of preaching. He also holds the honor of being the first African American to write and publish a full Bible commentary and study Bible, which was released in 2019.

For more information and a complimentary copy of Dr. Evans' devotional newsletter,

call: **(800) 800-3222**

or write:
TUA
PO Box 4000
Dallas, TX 75208

or visit: www.TonyEvans.org

NOTES:

1. "Church of the Nativity," *See the Holy Land*, accessed April 18, 2019, http://www.seetheholyland.net/church-of-the-nativity.

2. Ibid.

3. To learn more about Magdala, visit http://www.magdala.org.

4. "Stay Connected and Pray for the Peace of Jerusalem," *Love Israel,* accessed April 24, 2019, http://loveisrael.com.

NOTES:

. . . .
. . . .
. . . .
. . . .
. . . .
. . . .
. . . .
. . . .
. . . .
. . . .
. . . .
. . . .
. . . .
. . . .
. . . .
. . . .
. . . .
. . . .
. . . .
. . . .
. . . .